FROGS

What's inside?

World of frogs

Frogs belong to a group of animals called amphibians. Most frogs start life in water, then move on to dry land. Frogs come in many different colours and sizes. They can be as big as a football or as small as a grape.

Goliath frog

reed frog

Guess what?
Frogs live in most places, but you won't find them at the North or South poles, or in the sea.

edible frog
mantella frog
White's tree frog

Bullfrog

A bullfrog is a shy creature. When something scares it, this frog quickly hops away and hides. Adult bullfrogs live on land but they return to water to find a mate and to lay their eggs.

How loud?

A male bullfrog croaks to attract a mate. He puffs out his throat in a really big bubble and makes a noise that's as loud as a dog barking!

Bullfrog facts

All bullfrogs are big eaters. Usually, they feast on snails and insects, but a few gobble up bats and snakes.

Bullfrogs hate being cold. They spend the winter fast asleep under logs and stones. When it's warm and sunny, they come out again.

A bullfrog can gulp down lots of air and blow up its throat like a balloon. Hungry snakes are fooled into thinking that the frog is too big to eat!

From eggs to legs

Most frogs lay their eggs in water. The eggs hatch into wriggling tadpoles, which look a bit like fish. A tadpole slowly changes shape until it turns into a frog, just like its parents.

Growing up

A frog starts life as a tiny egg. As a frog grows up, it changes several times until it ends up looking completely different!

1 Egg

A frog lays lots of eggs. Each one is wrapped in a ball of jelly to keep it safe and warm.

2 to 3 days old

2 Tadpole

A young tadpole hatches from each egg. A tadpole has a long tail and breathes like a fish. Feathery gills on its head take in air from the water.

Making a splash

One kind of frog lays her eggs in a pool. If the pool dries out, the male digs a channel to a pond. When the eggs hatch, the tadpoles slide down the channel and splash into the water.

3 Froglet

The tadpole starts to grow legs and turn into a froglet. It also loses its gills and comes up to the water's surface to breathe.

4 Frog

The young frog's tail disappears and it looks just like its parents. Now the frog can live in or out of the water.

Guess what?
A few kinds of tadpoles take up to three years to turn into adult frogs.

Good fathers

A male Darwin's frog has a clever way of looking after his tadpoles. He keeps them in his throat until they grow into young frogs. Then they all hop out.

Poison dart frog

It's hard to believe that tiny poison dart frogs are among the most poisonous creatures on Earth. Many animals stay well away from these frogs because they know that their bright colours spell danger!

How poisonous?

This yellow-skinned poison dart frog is the most deadly of all. There is enough poison in the body of one frog to kill more than 50 snakes.

ha ha

What's a frog's favourite sweet?
A lolli-hop!

Poison dart frog facts

The poison dart frog deserves its scary name. People dip darts into the frog's poison to make deadly hunting weapons.

Like all frogs, poison dart frogs don't drink water, they take it in through their skin. If you gave them a glass of water, they would dive right in!

When a poison dart frog's eggs hatch, the mother frog carries her tadpoles to their own private swimming pool – in a water-filled plant!

What's for lunch?

Frogs are not fussy eaters. They snap up any animal they can fit into their mouths. Their favourite titbits are insects, worms, spiders and snails. A frog swallows its food whole, without biting or chewing.

Skin for dinner

From time to time, a frog sheds its skin to make room for the new one underneath. The old skin makes a tasty meal for the frog!

Sticky tongue

Most frogs have long, sticky tongues. A frog flicks out its tongue like a fishing line and catches a snack before the unlucky animal can escape.

Lucky leap

A leopard frog has really strong back legs for jumping. It leaps into the air and flicks out its tongue to catch insects as they fly past.

Guess what?
Some frogs don't have tongues. They cram food into their mouths with their front legs.

Open wide

A hungry horned frog needs a large lunch to fill its empty stomach. The frog's mouth is so wide that the frog can eat a mouse almost as big as itself.

Tree frog

Tree frogs are champion climbers. They have sticky pads on their feet to help them cling to branches. Often, a tiny tree frog is hard to spot because it blends in with the colour of the trees where it lives.

How old?

Frogs can live to a ripe old age. Some people keep White's tree frogs as pets. A few frogs have lived to be over 20 years old!

ha ha

Where do frogs keep their money?
In a river bank!

Tree frog facts

Tree frog tadpoles can ride piggy-back in a pouch on their mother's back.

Tree frogs like to hide in bunches of bananas. If the bananas are picked, the frogs can end up on a free trip around the world!

Most tree frogs are skinny, but the White's tree frog from Australia is the odd one out. This frog is big and fat!

AUSTRALIA

Hide and seek

Frogs come in many shapes, sizes, patterns and colours. They may be large and squat, or small and thin. Some are brightly coloured. Others blend in with their surroundings. A few frogs can even change colour.

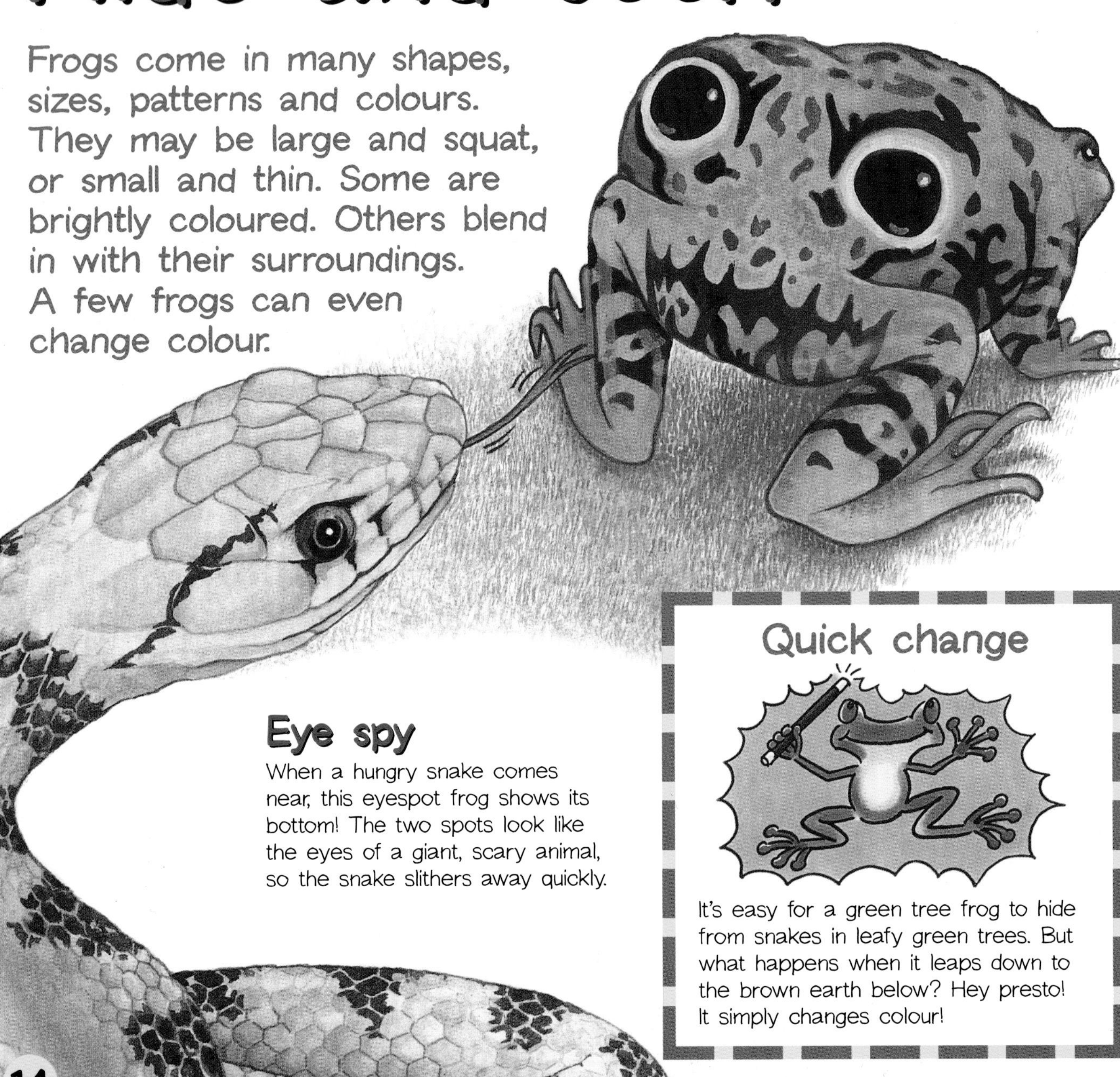

Eye spy

When a hungry snake comes near, this eyespot frog shows its bottom! The two spots look like the eyes of a giant, scary animal, so the snake slithers away quickly.

Quick change

It's easy for a green tree frog to hide from snakes in leafy green trees. But what happens when it leaps down to the brown earth below? Hey presto! It simply changes colour!

See-through skin

A glass frog has greenish see-through skin that helps it to hide on leaves and branches in the rainforest.

Guess what?
A few frogs with bright red eyes can even see in the dark.

Leafy disguise

This Malayan horned frog looks like a dead leaf on the forest floor. Here, it hides from hungry enemies, or lies in wait for a yummy snack.

Hop to it

Frogs move around in all sorts of ways. There are frogs that climb trees and others that burrow underground. Many frogs have huge webbed feet that help them swim in water or glide through the air.

Guess what?
A few frogs can hop as far as 5 metres. That's half the width of a tennis court!

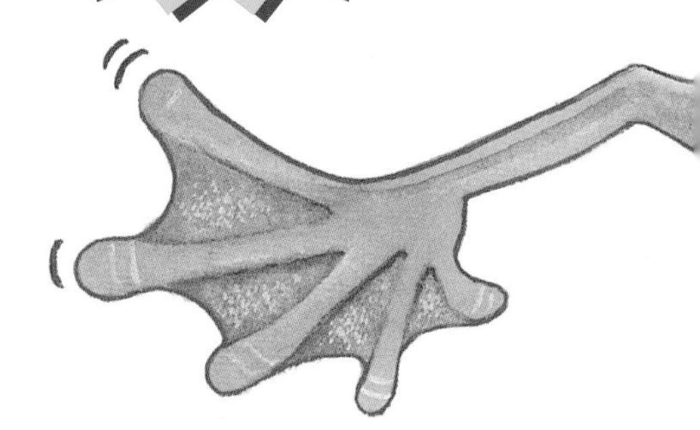

Super swimmer

This frog is a fantastic swimmer. It moves by kicking out its powerful back legs and webbed feet. The frog feels for rocks and plants with its front legs.

Great glider

Gliding frogs seem to fly as they leap from tree to tree. They cover great distances in just a single jump.

Digging dynamo

The Australian burrowing frog is an expert digger. It burrows underground to make a cool shelter where it can hide from the blazing desert sun.

Cool climber

This tree frog from North America is great at climbing. Its long toes grip the slippery branches tightly so that it doesn't slide off.

A LESSON IN FROG LANGUAGE
CROAK
CROAK
On spring evenings, you can often hear frogs croaking around ponds. Frogs don't just croak for fun. It's their way of talking.

1
Usually, a male frog croaks to attract females. The frog with the loudest, longest croak is the most popular.
CROAK
CROAK

2
A choir of male frogs gathers together and croaks in harmony. Female frogs have no voices or very quiet ones, so they just listen.

5

This frog's croak can't be heard over the noisy waterfalls, where it lives. So the frog sends signals by waving a bright blue foot in the air.

HELLO

TIME TO GO

Fast facts

Here, you can find out amazing facts about some of the frogs you have already met.

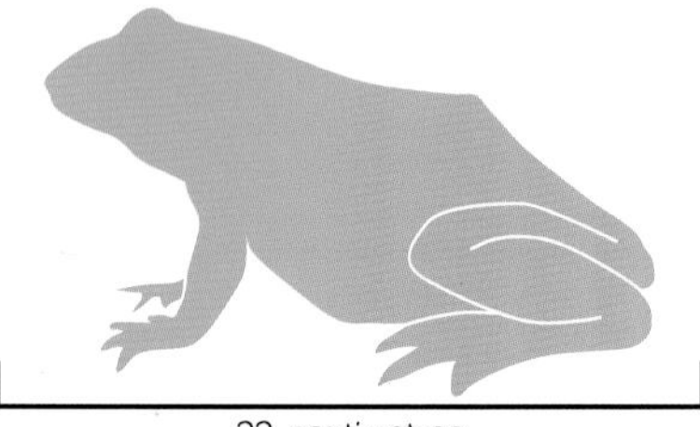

Poison dart frog

Favourite food: ants and other insects
Colour: many bright colours – some are also patterned.
Home: rainforests of Central and South America.
Worst enemy: these frogs have few enemies because they are so poisonous.
Interesting fact: a poison dart frog carries its tadpoles piggy-back style to a new home.

Goliath frog

Favourite food: mice and lizards
Colour: greenish-brown
Home: deep forest pools in West Africa.
Worst enemy: people who hunt and eat Goliath frogs.
Interesting fact: the Goliath frog is the biggest frog in the world. It can weigh more than 3.2 kilogrammes. That's as much as a newborn human baby.

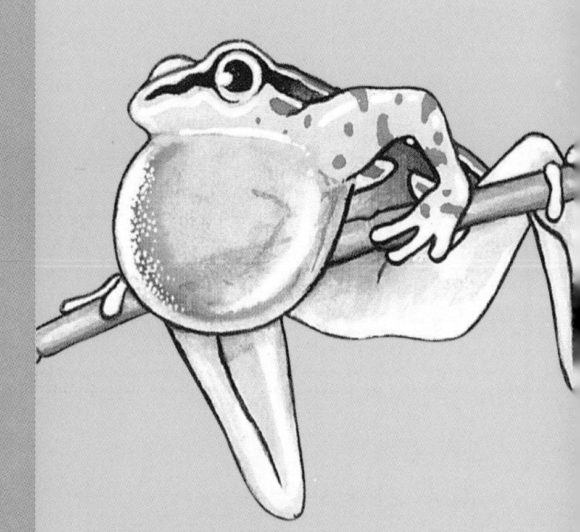

Reed frog

Favourite food: insects
Colour: many different colours. Some have spots and stripes, others have gold and silver patterns.
Home: reedy lakes, ponds and swamps in Africa.
Worst enemies: birds, lizards and snakes
Interesting fact: male reed frogs can croak really loudly. They can be heard over 3 kilometres away.

20.3 centimetres
bullfrog

20.3 centimetres
Australian burrowing frog

6.3 centimetres
tree frog

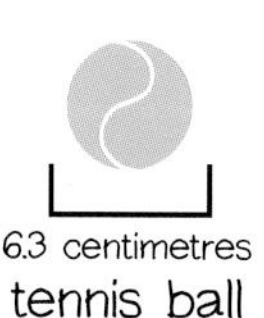

6.3 centimetres
tennis ball

3.8 centimetres
reed frog

2.5 centimetres
poison dart frog

Australian burrowing frog

Favourite food: insects
Colour: speckled greenish brown or pink.
Home: baking-hot sandy deserts in Australia.
Worst enemy: people who live in the desert and who squeeze water out of the frog's body to drink.
Interesting fact: in dry weather, this frog lives on water stored inside its body.

Bullfrog

Favourite food: frogs, snakes and even birds.
Colour: greenish-brown with speckles on its back.
Home: swamps and lakes in North America.
Worst enemy: people who disturb the places where these frogs live.
Interesting fact: bullfrogs can grow big enough to fill a large dinner plate.

Tree frog

Favourite food: insects
Colour: green or brown. Some have red eyes.
Home: trees and bushes in North, Central and South America. They also live in Australia.
Worst enemy: snakes
Interesting fact: the pads on a tree frog's feet are so sticky that the frog can climb up a shiny window pane.

Puzzles

Here are some puzzles to try. Look back in the book to help you find the answers.

Close-up!

We've zoomed in on some frogs that you met earlier. Can you tell which ones they are?

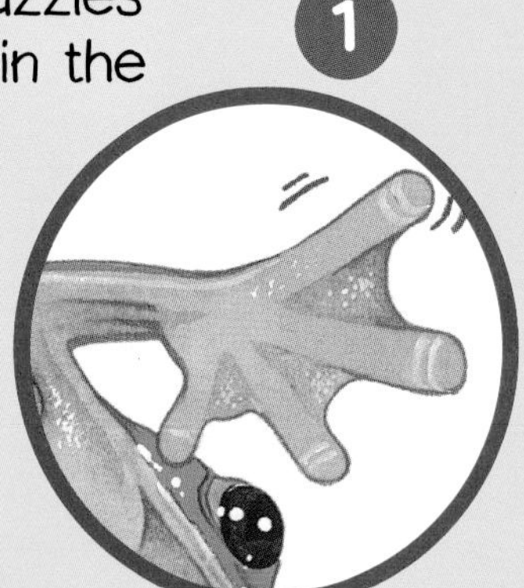

Hide and seek

There are five frogs hiding in this picture. Can you find them?

Spot the difference

Look carefully at these poison dart frogs. Can you spot four differences between the pictures?

Home sweet home

These three frogs are trying to find their way home. Can you help them?

Answers

Close-up! 1. gliding frog page 17, 2. eyespot frog page 14, 3. Malayan horned frog page 15

Hide and seek on the lily pad, behind the stones, in the water, on the log, in the reeds

Spot the difference Picture b: frog is not flicking its tongue, one toe is missing, frog's spots are yellow, one fly is missing

Home sweet home Australian burrowing frog – desert, bullfrog – pond, glass frog – rainforest

Index

Published by
Two-Can Publishing
A division of Zenith Entertainment plc
43-45 Dorset Street
London W1H 4AB

Created by
Two-Can Design Ltd
346 Old Street
London EC1V 9RB

Main illustrations: Miles Changeur
Cartoon illustrations: Alan Rowe
Consultants: Dr Barry Clarke and Anna Keen
Photographs: front cover BBC Natural History Unit/Phil Savoie; p4 Bruce Coleman Ltd; p8 Michael and Patricia Fogden; p12 NHPA.

ISBN 1-85434-802-7

Dewey Decimal Classification 597.8

Paperback 10 9 8 7 6 5 4 3 2 1

A catalogue record for this book is available from the British Library

Printed in Hong Kong by Wing King Tong